Foundations in Pattaya

Giving Back to Thailand

By

Balthazar Moreno

Published by <u>nocovercharge.com</u> 2012

This book is available on Kindle Amazon
Official Facebook Page: http://www.facebook.com/PattayaFoundations
Official Website: http://www.donate2thailand.com
Facebook Website Page: http://www.facebook.com/DonateThailand
Internet Publisher: http://www.nocovercharge.com
Facebook Page: http://www.facebook.com/nocovercharge
Twitter: @ThailandBooks

Other books Published by No Cover Charge Available on Amazon over the list of books
Discover Thailand Miracles Series Volume 1-9
99 Things to do in Pattaya Kindle ASIN:B007JFMGMO/
Books ISBN-13:978-1477418949 ISBN-10:1477418946
Pattaya Beach Secrets Hidden Beaches in Thailand Kindle ASIN:B007QI4ZPK/
Books ISBN-13:978-1477428801 ISBN-10:1477428801
Amazing Museums in Pattaya Kindle ASIN:B007QS02XY/
Books ISBN-13:978-1477419137 ISBN-10:1477419136
Pattaya Sport & Activities Kindle ASIN:B007QSC1O2/
Books ISBN-13:978-1477428948 ISBN-10:1477428941
Pattaya Nature Trails Secret Waterfall Kindle ASIN:B007R0RW84/
Books ISBN-13:978-1477428863 ISBN-10:1477428860
Newbie Guide to Pattaya Attractions Kindle ASIN:B007R16UTA/
Books ISBN-13:978-1477428771 ISBN-10:1477428771
Pattaya Secret Temples Discover Thailand Kindle ASIN:B007R7KHMK/
Books ISBN-13:978-1477428917 ISBN-10:1477428917
Newbie Guide to Pattaya Entertainment Kindle ASIN:B007R9F3ZO/
Books ISBN-13:978-1477428795 ISBN-10:1477428798
Pattaya Hidden Island's Kindle ASIN:B007R1GCSE/
Books ISBN-13:978-1477428856 ISBN-10:1477428852

Thailand Shopping Series Volume 1
Best Deal's in Pattaya Kindle ASIN:B007QUXIF6/
Books ISBN-13:978-1477428672 ISBN-10:1477428674

Thailand Business & Property Series Volume 1
Avoid Property Scams in Thailand Kindle ASIN:B007QSKHAM/
Books ISBN-13:978-1477419403 ISBN-10:1477419403

Thailand Health & Wellness Series Volume 1
Sexually Transmitted Diseases in Thailand Kindle ASIN:B007R9F1PG/
Books ISBN-13:978-1477428962 ISBN-10:1477428968

Helping Others Charities & Foundations Volume 1
Foundations in Pattaya Giving Back to Thailand Kindle ASIN:B007R7SUD8/
Books ISBN-13:978-1477428726 ISBN-10:1477428720
Natural Health & Wellness Series Volume 1
The Complete Guide to Natural Remedies for STD-STI Kindle ASIN:B007QIMCVO/
Books ISBN-13:978-1477428979 ISBN-10:1477428976

Disclaimer

A lot of care has been taken in the accuracy of information provided in this book; however, it cannot be guaranteed that inaccuracies will not occur. The Copyright owner cannot be held responsible for any claims for damages caused as a result of any error of this book. We do not guarantee that any of these foundations live up to your standards. We all have different values and moral codes and picking is totally in your discretion.

Dedication

I want to dedicate this book to Buddhism and the Lord Buddha for his teachings. For true Buddhism charity comes naturally. If you are a follower of the lord Buddha's teachings, the act of giving to others will come to you as something as natural as breathing.

Preface

Pattaya is mostly known to be a fun playground for most people who come and never see its dark side. Like any other fun filled affair, it should come with a hangover. It can be argued that Pattaya is experiencing a massive hang over and it can be seen if one will linger a bit more to see it closely.

Many girls in Pattaya are addicted to various things such as alcohol, illegal drugs, forms of medication, among other vices that it is safe to say that they are mentally burned out. Most of these girls came from broken families and thus live chaotic and unsupervised day to day living. When they are not staying in posh five star hotels with guests, they stay in bad apartments.

The booming property industry mostly consists of shiny apartments and new houses everywhere you look. But at the back are workers from Burma and Cambodia working for as low as 2 USD a day, with no insurance while carrying the risk of getting sent back without salary.

Like in any other countries, homeless children and elders are present in Pattaya. These children come from dead parents while some are simply extremely poor and the rest are runaway kids. As if it is not enough, some of these children have HIV while the others are handicapped. The Thai government is doing whatever it can while the rest is done by foundations.

Should you wish to help Pattaya, please feel free to take a look at any of the foundations listed in this book? As always, when it comes to supporting charities and foundations, one should use his or her better judgment. Books, food, toys and volunteer work are way better than cash in hand. In any case charities refuse to receive the forms of help mentioned and ask for money instead, we encourage turning away and reporting the charity to us.

These are NOT ALL charities in Pattaya and we will try to add more charities as we find them. Some charities are too small while some only talk in Thai language. If you register on the bonus forum we will keep you updates on new versions of the book. If you know any other charities in Pattaya, please let us know.

Prologue

Pattaya

Pattaya is for some people heaven on earth while for others it is a place they do not even consider visiting. It used to be a small fishing village in the 1960s but now one of the biggest tourist attractions in Thailand. The heart of Pattaya is located about two hours from Bangkok and an hour from Thailand National Airport by car.

Pattaya is ever growing

Pattaya is continuously growing and its property market is probably bigger than Phuket, Samui and Krabi combined. When people now talk about Pattaya, they also include the beaches of Bans ray and Wonga mat on the other side. Many of the Pattaya expats are working in the property market and it is probably the biggest work sector after being a bar owner.

The inhabits of Pattaya

Although the Americans were the ones who started the Pattaya's boom after coming from Vietnam, the British and Scandinavians eventually took over. Over time, Other Europeans such as the French, Germans and the Swiss followed through. This influx became the norm for a good while until the Russian invasion came about in 2010. Hordes after hordes came that they are now the fastest growing inhabits in Pattaya. They have their visa upon arrival; get a direct flight to the Utapao Airport just outside Pattaya. As a result of this massive Russian influx, many local shops exclusively have Russian language on their doors and menus while the City Hall of Pattaya offers free Russian language lessons. Aside from Russians, Pattaya also had a huge influx of Arab and Indian tourists since 2010 onwards however; they just go for a few weeks of vacation. After the 2011 flood in Bangkok and the northeast Thailand, many Bangkokians bought houses or apartments in Pattaya. In lieu to this, we would probably see a greater influx of Thais calling Pattaya home over the years.

The weather in Pattaya

The weather is mostly composed of a tropical dry and wet climate which is divided into seasons following a normal pattern that goes warm and dry (November to February), hot and humid (March to May) and hot and rainy (June to October). Due to environmental issues which affect the entire world, the climate sometimes has slight alterations. When Bangkok was flooded for a month, Pattaya only had it for a day. It normally does not rain in Pattaya while days of rain are experienced in Bangkok.

Five star Pattaya

Pattaya is rich in five star establishments. There are a few five star hospitals, a number of five star hotels and a central shopping center that just opened in 2010 aside from the already long existing five star properties all over Pattaya as well as numerous fine dining restaurants and international bars. The Thai people who govern Pattaya are trying to create a more posh and upscale Pattaya but only the future can tell how much they will succeed.

The backside of Pattaya

Even if the newly elected mayor Pattaya Khun Itipon trying to fix the problems he cannot fix all problems at once or even ever. The Police are not under the control of Khun Itipon and lately the big influx of Russian has created totally new criminals gangs in Pattaya outside the control of the Police. Many poor people from the countryside see Pattaya as the place they can get rich quick but most of them ends up broke. Regardless of how much Pattaya tries to hide it, it is still suffering from problems such as drugs, prostitution, among other crimes and here are some pointers to keep you safe.

Some Safety Advice

Bag and necklace snatchers

Mostly these motorbike gangs snatch gold chains while tourist riding motorbike or even a tuk tuk, leave your big gold chain at home.

Bag snatching is more rare but happens mostly late at night when someone passes out. Pickpockets Sadly to say ladyboys overrepresented and most of the crimes happens when a group of ladyboys trying to touch male walking by. While the male victim is trying to protect his private parts the ladyboys takes his wallet or phone. Also watch out for the small begging children hugging you late at night on Walking Street.

Robberies

Street hold ups or mugging are rare and unless you flashing money around and walking in the slum area you are fine. There are many security guards all around Pattaya, guarding everything from ATM to hotels.

Thieves

Do not trust the lock on your door in the hotel or even the safe. Gangs from outside Thailand have targeted some hotels in Pattaya because they use bad safes that are easy to open. We also followed many cases in the news of staff stealing belongings in the hotel and most of the time the hotel sides with the staff. Check Trip advisor or Thailandscam.com for warnings about hotels that never fire staff that steals.

If you take friends to your room make sure the guest show ID at the reception.

Health

Careful when you eat seafood or salad in Pattaya or the rest of Thailand it can make you very sick. Some restaurants lack proper hygiene since they just cater tourist and do not really care if tourist come back or not. Also mind the hot climate and make sure you step up the level of water you drink. The reputation that many people get drugged is just not true; it is most likely jet lag and drinking too much.

Sex Just use your common sense and remember a girl, boy or ladyboy that sell sex is a prostitute even in Thailand and would you date a prostitute in your home country?

Drugs

Do not be fooled by the lazy look of the Thai police, undercover police and snitches are plentiful. The police sometimes have road blocks and everybody including tourists need to take a piss in a glass, if you have drugs in your blood you are in trouble. From 2012 the police also have roadblocks to check for Alcohol in your system, if they catch you they can send you to prison right away.

Traffic

USA called Thailand the second dangerous country when it comes to traffic accidents and they are not joking. Be very careful when driving or as a passenger, if the driver drives too fast ask him to slow down (in Thai Jen Jen).

Traveling to Pattaya

By car: If you have your own car you can be reached about 2 hours from Bangkok. Just follow the highway leading to Chonburi and Si Racha. There is an also a road under the highway but if can be a difficult to find.

By bus: Most people take the Air-conditioned and regular buses depart from the Eastern Bus Terminal (Ekkamai). You can also use Bangkok's Northern Bus Terminal (Mochit 2 Bus Terminal). Price is around 120 THB and busses run from 05.00-22.00.

By bus airport: There are buses leaving from the airport from 08.00-20.00 everyday.

By Train: For those who want to see something new (or rather old) The State Railway of Thailand offers a daily train service departing Bangkok's Hua Lamphong Station at 06:55 a.m. Not recommended for first time travelers with excessive luggage.

By Taxi: You can stop a taxi at most places in Bangkok and ask the driver to take you to Pattaya, the price will range from 1000-2000 THB with toll way.

By Van: For the more experienced travelers there is Van services all over Bangkok but they do not speak English and change time and place.

By Air: Bangkok Airways provides daily flights connecting Ko Samui and U-Taphao Airport. (Approximately 30 kilometers south of Pattaya).

Traveling in Pattaya city

Pattaya City has song taew (a pickup with a roof) but most people called them Tuk Tuk they have special routes and you pay 10-20 THB each route. You can also rent them as normal taxis for a fixed price if they have no passengers. Since 2011 Pattaya City has had metered Taxis but they never use meters and are overpriced.

Cars can be rented for 1000 THB a day and motorbikes for 300 THB. One is strongly encouraged to make sure that these operators have insurance for their cars. Although some websites will claim that one does not need a driver's license, it is completely false. The police will ask for your license in any case they stop you on the road. However, one's license from his or her country may be used for a period of 60 days.

Contents

CHAPTER ONE:

BOOK FOR CHARITY

This book was solely written for charity and thus all profits that will be generated from this book will be offered to charity. Please visit our website http://www.donate2thailand.com to get a chance to vote on which charities the proceeds should be given to and to inquire about other methods that will enable you to help. So it is really up to you, if you borrowed or download the book for free maybe you should buy it as well? WE ALL NEED TO THRIVE.

CHAPTER TWO:

FOUNDATION

Karunyawet Home for the Disabled

Karunyawet Foundation For Persons with Disabilities or KFPWD. Assistance in helping disadvantaged people with disabilities.

Karunyawet Foundation is open daily from 08:00 am. – 06:30 pm.

A foundation not so well know as the other foundations it always welcomes visitors.

Contact:
Address: 105 M.3, Sukhumvit Rd., Banglamung, Chonburi 20150
Telephone: +66 3824 1741-2
Website: http://www.karunyawet.go.th

Father Ray Foundation

The Father Ray Foundation is named after Father Raymond Brennan. The Foundation cares for more than 850 children without a family, street children, blind children and young disabled adults. The vision is "We Never Turn a Needy Child Away".

The Father Ray Foundation was founded in 2003 by Father Raymond Allen Brennan, C.Ss.R., a Catholic Priest of the Redemptory's Order in Thailand. It is a charitable organization set up to make a positive difference in the lives of underprivileged children, young people with disabilities and the poor of Thailand.

Father Raymond Brennan was a Redemptory's priest born in the USA who in 1972 was requested to assist at the local church, St. Nikolas church, Pattaya. One day a young Thai lady approached Fr. Ray and asked if he could take care of her baby as she had married (not to the father of the baby) and the husband wanted nothing to do with the child. The baby was taken in and as the word got around about Fr. Ray's generosity and caring more young children were brought to him and that was the beginning. Most of the children presented to Father Ray were the offspring of Thai women and US servicemen who were stationed at the US military base at Satanic during the Vietnam War.

Father Ray grew concerned about the sudden boom in "war babies" and began to visit the US military in Thailand in the hope of finding ways and means of aid to care for the children. Father Ray held meetings with several officers in the army which resulted in representatives from the army and Father Ray himself visiting Bishop Thienchai Samanchit, the Bishop of the Chanthaburi Diocese at the bishop's house, Si Racha. During these visits, Father Ray informed the bishop that the American veterans wanted to build a home for the children in Pattaya and present it to the Diocese, of which Father Ray Brennan would be the manager. Fully aware of the task ahead Bishop Thienchai Samanchit replied, "It is not difficult for you to build a home for orphans and then wash your hand and go home, while it is not known where the Diocese will get money from to feed those orphans".

Construction of an orphanage began immediately and on October 24, 1978, the governor of Chonburi Province issued the Pattaya Orphanage establishment license. Official adoption was granted on March 27, 1981, when permission was received for the orphanage "to be a child welfare organization operating for the adoption of both Thai and foreign children." Through the years, Father Ray responded to the needs of children and young people in Pattaya. Since his passing in 2003, the Foundation has continued to care for children in Pattaya in his memory with the Father Ray Children's Village and the Father Ray Day Care Center. The Father Ray Foundation is open daily from 08:00 am. – 06:00 pm.

Contact:
Address: 440 M.9, Sukhumvit Rd., Nongprue, Banglamung, Chonburi 20260
Telephone: +66 3871 6628
Website: http://www.fr-ray.org

Mercy Center Pattaya

The work of Mercy began in the year 2000 with our growing desire to help the "street children" of Pattaya. There are the hundreds (perhaps thousands) of children and youth who live most of their young lives "at risk", as a result of direct abuse, severe neglect, or the danger of being swallowed up in the life threatening environment of crime, drugs and sexual abuse that surrounds them on a daily basis.

There are the hundreds (perhaps thousands) of children and youth who live most of their young lives "at risk" as a result of direct abuse, severe neglect, or the danger of being swallowed up in the life threatening environment of crime, drugs and sexual abuse that surrounds them on a daily basis.

Mercy Center Pattaya Project:

Children's home: children's home / shelter protects and provides for children who are "at risk" in our community, because of either of direct abuse or abuse by severe neglect. MERCY's team of dedicated care-givers provide a clean, safe, home, good food, medical care, clothing, education and lots of love to all the children.

Chumchon (Slums) Project: Each week the MERCY team goes into Pattaya most destitute areas to bring basic food items, clothes, milk for the children, emergency medical care as needed, and hope to some of Pattaya poorest residents.

Scholarship Project: With financial support from local and international sponsors, MERCY provides scholarships for over 220 + needy Thai students, who are referred by local school authorities or Chumchon (slum) community leaders.

Prisons: Three times a week, a team of MERCY staff and volunteers take fruit, clean drinking water and sandwiches (when supplies are available) to people in local police lock-up centers. MERCY offers emergency care as needed, help contacting family or embassies (if foreigners), and family support if Thai nationals.

Micro Enterprise and Livelihood and Community Development: Individual gifts or loans (as appropriate) are given to specific individuals to help create financial independence in the lives of the poorest of the poor.

Early Learning Center: Created to provide a positive learning environment for children in Chumchon airat (slum) areas. These centers prevent children from 3 months old and up from being left in circumstances where they are put 'at risk'

Mercy Center Pattaya is open daily from 09:00 am. – 05:00 pm.

Contact:

Address:	565/55 M.10, Nongprue, Banglamung, Chonburi 20150
Telephone:	+66 3841 6707
Website:	http://mercypattaya.com

Pattaya Orphanage

In 1972, Rev. Fr. Raymond Allyn Brennan, a Redemptory's priest, was requested to go to help work at St. Nikolas Church, Pattaya, temporarily, and one morning when he opened the church door he saw a newborn child left at the stairway front. Not knowing what to do, he took care of the child, asking his friends about "how to give milk and how to change the diaper". News about the fostering of the child spread, resulting in more children being brought to give to him, most of who were fruits of the presence of the U.S. military base at Sattahip.

During the Vietnam War, Pattaya became a favorite place of the American servicemen who came for recreations, so there were a large number of abandoned children. A military officer and Father Ray consulted each other on how to find ways and means of aid. Eventually, both of them went to see Bishop Thienchai Samanchit, the Bishop of the Chanthaburi Diocese at the Bishop's House, Siracha, informing him that the American veterans intended to build a home for orphans at Pattaya and present it to the Diocese, of which Father Ray Brennan volunteered to be the manager, since it was found that many orphans were born of American servicemen in the days of their presence at U-Tapao U.S. base during the Vietnam War.

Bishop Thienchai answered the American military officer, saying, "It is not difficult for you to build a home for orphans and then wash your hand and go home, while it is not known where the Diocese will get money from to feed those orphans". So he asked for an initial capital of Baht 500,000 (Baht Five Hundred Thousand Only). The American military officer nodded approval but asked for 5 years' time.

Thereafter, Bishop Thienchai took counsel with his advisors as to whether or not to accept the Pattaya Orphanage. Some of the advisors raised an objection, saying that the orphanage should not be constructed, because it was like supporting the easy existence of a growing number of orphans. Some of them said that even if the orphanage did not exist, there were already a large number of orphans. Eventually, the Diocese passed a resolution accepting the Pattaya Orphanage to belong to the Diocese. Father Ray and the American servicemen constructed the orphanage on a land (of approximately 7.6 acres) of the Diocese, of which the Diocese prescribed 2 acres on the rear side for use as the compound of the orphanage. Brother Connie of the Redemptory's Order was the construction drawing maker, while the Diocese reserved 5.6 acres of the land on the road front side.

In the initial period Father Ray contacted the Sisters (Soeurs) of the Order of St. Paul de Chartre to come to be housekeepers looking after the children.

On October 24, 1978, the Governor of Chonburi Province issued the Pattaya Orphanage establishment license.

On March 1, 1979, Bishop Thienchai contacted the Sisters of the Order of Lovers of the Cross of Chanthaburi to come to perform the duties in place to date.

On January 9, 1981, the National Cultural Commission Secretary General issued the Pattaya Orphanage organization license.

On March 27, 1981, permission was received to be a child welfare organization operating for the adoption of both Thai and foreign children.

About us: History of Pattaya Orphanage:

When the 5-year schedule fell due, the American veterans collected the amount of Baht 500,000 to give to the Pattaya Orphanage as they had promised.

In 1995, a 3-storey building was constructed as the lodging or boys and mentors.

In 1999, a 5-storey building was constructed as a learning place of Sot Pattana (Audio Development) Kindergarten for deaf children and as the lodging of both male and female small orphans.

In 2001, a 2-storey building was constructed, the lower floor being the dining hall, the upper floor being the multi-purpose meeting hall, the last piece of construction for the Pattaya Orphanage.

In 2003, after Father Ray's death, Father Banchong Chaiyara and Father Larry Patin subsequently managed the work of the orphanage.

In 2006, the first building was overhauled.

It had been until January 1, 2008 when the Chanthaburi Diocese assigned Father Michael Weera Phangrak to be the Pattaya Orphanage Director and Father Kritsada Sukkaphat, the Deputy Director.

Currently the Pattaya Orphanage takes care of approximately 180 orphans, ranging from newborn to studying at the university level.

Contact:

Address:	384 M.6, Sukhumvit Highway Km.144, Naklua, Banglamung, Chonburi 20150
Telephone:	+66 3842 3468, +66 3841 6426
Website:	http://www.thepattayaorphanage.org

The Jesters Care for Kids

The Jesters Care for Kids Charity Drive was established in 1998 to provide children in need with educational opportunities for a brighter future.

"We are a children's charity who help children of all ages, including disabled children, orphaned children, abandoned children, underprivileged children and local schools. With our help they lead a happier, more comfortable life with a promising future."

Education: Children born into impoverished conditions often do not have the means or documentation to attend school. Our target charity, The Fountain of Life Center for Children, under the auspices of the Good Shepherd Foundation, visits the villages of these children and obtains identities. After preschool orientation, scholarships are made available so they may attend government schools.

Shelter: Orphaned, abandoned street kids are at risk to sexual predators and drug abuse. Other kids are born with HIV/AIDS and their families and communities are unable to care for them. For these reasons, we also support Baan Jing Jai Orphanage and the Camillian Home for their invaluable care for children living with HIV/AIDS.

Special Schools and Needs: They assist the Pattaya Redemptory's School for the Blind, Khao Baisri Special Education 12 for the disabled. Share Love with a Friend distributes rice to families with disabled kids, and provides wheelchairs and walkers.

Contact:
Address: 3/199 M.6 Soi Chalermprakiet 3, Pattaya 3rd Rd., Naklua, Banglamung,
               Chonburi 20150
Telephone: +66(0)38-361 720
Website: http://www.care4kids.info

Fountain of Life Children's Center

Many poor families from the Northeast of Thailand come to Pattaya to seek a better life. The reality for many is to earn a meager living as street vendors or garbage collectors. In these types of communities, drug & alcohol abuse is common.

Slum dwellings are without the benefits of house registration which is needed to access healthcare and education. Births are often not registered so the children are undocumented and without civil rights.

The children suffer from lack of care, poor hygiene and malnutrition resulting in poor general health, stunted growth and tooth decay.

Often families break up and the children are left to be cared for by elderly relatives. They lose their sense of identity and self worth.

Many of them know only their nickname and not their family name nor date of birth. Uneducated parents often do not realize the value of education and keep their children home.

Children with opportunities are children with a future.

Priority is given to obtaining the children's birth certificates to enable them to enter government schools when they are seven years old.

We give financial support when needed to buy uniforms and to cover lunch and transportation costs. Some of the families would not be able to send their children to school without this help. The children are supported throughout their education if necessary, so each year we help more and more children.

At the center, the children receive not only a basic education but also learn about their culture so that they can be accepted into Thai society.

Poverty is the enemy of these children and education the best weapon to fight it.

Our caring staff monitors the children's health and physical and emotional well being. Minor illnesses are treated at the center and sick children are taken for hospital appointments, and surgery, if needed. Many children require extensive dental treatment so visits to the dentist are of paramount importance.

There are a growing number of older children who come to the center. Some have never been to school or have been unable to maintain their studies. They are encouraged to study for their Primary certificate and vocational training.

These are our most challenging children and need great patience, love and understanding. Regular group and individual counseling is a vital part of their development. Along with health education they are taught about their rights, especially regarding child abuse and child labor laws.

To motivate these teenagers to attend regularly we organize outings and sport activities. Local and International schools are involved in the spirit of 'kids helping kids'.

Once a week, a group of volunteers work with the children to make greetings cards. The profits from selling them are paid into the children's credit union and they can withdraw cash once a week. This teaches them how to manage money and gives them a sense of independence.

Great effort is made to obtain ID cards for them when they are 15. Life would be particularly difficult without one.

Scholarships are available for those who wish to further their education and, one day, realize their dreams.

Contact:
Address: 3/199 M.6, Naklua, Banglamung, Chonburi 20150
Telephone: +66 3836 1720
Website: http://www.fountainoflifepattaya.com

Pattaya Redemptorist Vocational School for the Blind

A committee has recently been established to help complete 17th February Pattaya School for the Blind building due to a shortage of funds, which has delayed its completion.

A meeting was held at the Woodlands Suites Serviced Residence Suites in Pattaya recently to explore ways of raising funds to complete the new building at the Pattaya Blind School, the construction of which has begun but had to be slowed down due to budget constraints.

At the meeting Sven Philip Sorensen, advisor to the Swedish Executive Scout Board was unanimously elected as Chairman. Other committee members appointed to help facilitate the completion of the building project were: Sutham Phanthusak - deputy chairman, Pratheep Malhotra - secretary & public relations, Stephane Bringer - assistant secretary, Alisa Phanthusak - treasurer, Jan Olav Aamlid - fund raising, Suchai Rujivanitchkul - director in charge of construction, Father Lawrence Patin - director of Fr.Ray Foundation and Aurora Sribuaphan - director of the Pattaya School of the Blind.

To understand the purpose of the project, Aurora Sribuaphan, director of the Pattaya Blind School informed the committee that the Pattaya Redemptorist School for the Blind, under the patronage of Her Royal Highness Princess Maha Chakri Sirindhorn, was licensed by the congregation of the Most Blessed Redeemer in Thailand to construct two buildings for teaching blind people.

She said, "Part of the budget for the two buildings being constructed came from money donated through the HRH Princess Foundation which was established after HRH Princess Maha Chakri Sirindhorn came to inaugurate the school building in 1993 and donated 5,000 baht towards the development of education for the blind. The school used that amount to set up the foundation with the aim of receiving donations from kind-hearted people.

"The two buildings to be connected in an L shape consist of the HRH Princess Sirindhorn Building, completed with a budget of 17 million baht and the Father Ray Building now under construction at a cost of 14 million baht."

Sven said, "Construction of the second building has begun and the building itself has been completed at a cost of 7 million baht. The second phase of architectural work requires a total of another seven million baht or one million baht for each floor of the seven-story building. But due to lack of funds, construction and completion of the interior had to be postponed until more money could be raised to complete the project."

Sven asked the committee to help find generous donors saying, "Initially we sought 7 donors of US $30,000 (one million baht) for each floor. The good news is that when Honorary President of the World Scout Foundation, His Majesty King Carl XVI Gustaf of Sweden visited the Pattaya Blind School on February 17, 2009, to inspect the school's scouting educational course and to induct blind children into the scout movement, he was invited to inspect the construction site of the new building. The benevolent King understood the urgency of the need to finish the project, so together with HM Queen Sylvia pledged US$30,000 from Her Majesty's very own "Queen Silvia Fund" towards the building project. The fund is operated by the World Scout Foundation which raises funds for Scouts with disabilities. HM Queen Sylvia is scheduled to preside over the official opening of the building in October this year.

The visit by His Majesty King Carl XVI Gustaf of Sweden was initiated by Sutham Phanthusak, managing director of the Woodland Hotel & Resort and international commissioner of the National Scouts Organization of Thailand who is also a staunch supporter of the School for the Blind.

Sutham said, "I have always dreamed that the blind scouts would come under the patronage of His Majesty King Carl XVI Gustaf of Sweden." Together with Sven Philip Sorensen, a close friend of HM King Carl XVI Gustaf, they worked together to make this dream come true. "It was a proud moment for all of us, especially the blind children when His Majesty presented scouting scarves and caps to the blind scouts that day."

Sven added, "Since then there have been other groups and individual generous donations received to complement the funds already raised, but we still don't have enough."

Sutham has put out a plea to the Pattaya community and service organizations to help in raising at least one million baht to complete one floor of the school. "If the people and service and charity organizations in and around Pattaya can set aside a small budget from their fund raising programs, I am confident that we can 'Make Dreams Real' for the blind children not only in Pattaya but for children all over Thailand," he said.

Sutham went on to say, "There are not enough schools for blind children in Thailand, so the Pattaya School for the blind receives children from all over the country. What we are trying to achieve here will benefit thousands of these unfortunate children. Please help them as much as you can."

Update of the construction and information will be posted on the Pattaya Redemptorist School for the Blind website (www. pattayablind.org) with a link which will feature the story: "HM King Carl XVI Gustaf of Sweden inducts Cub Scouts at the Blind School, Pattaya."

Contact:
Address: 285/103 M.5, Soi 16, Nongprue, Banglamung, Chonburi 20150
Telephone: +66 3822 5479, +66 3822 5963
Website: http://www.pattayablind.org

Baanjingjai Foundation

Baan Jing Jai currently cares for around 70 children and adolescents aged 1 to 18 years. Most of the children's parents are dead or have drug and/or mental issues. In the 11 years since the orphanage was founded the numbers of children taken into care has grown as has the monthly bills to take care of their food, education and associated costs of living. There are 4 permanent staff and 6 volunteers who work around the clock.

Contact:
Address: 82/1 M.6, Nongprue, Banglamung, Chonburi, 20150
Telephone: +66 3873 0125, +66 084 614 4389, +66 089 678 7041
Website: http://www.baanjingjai.org

Share Love with a Friend

Sam Somkiat is a Thai national who is committed to caring for the needs of the disabled children in the Pattaya area. Having contracted polio as a child, he is in a wheelchair himself and he understands the needs and difficulties of disabled people firsthand.

Once a month, Sam distributes rice to these children and their families. Taking care of a disabled child can be quite costly and this donation of rice makes a big difference to these families. Each family receives 2-3 bags of rice (5 kg) costing approximately 150 Baht (about US$5) per bag.

It is important that these children receive good quality soft rice as often swallowing food is very difficult. The cheaper hard rice can be dangerous for them to consume.

Contact:
Address: 20/149 M.10, Soi Day Night, Nongprue, Banglamung, Chonburi 20150
Telephone: +66 90 767 1939
Website: http:// www.sharelovewithafriend.org

The Glory Hut Foundation

The purpose of the foundation:

- To contribute to communities. Those with family problems. Poor families. Vulnerable groups of society.
- In order to help develop and enhance skills in various aspects of life. Through the consultation process from a social worker. Or psychologist. Vocational training to encourage employment. Provide health counseling to people with AIDS. Or sexually transmitted diseases. Assistance to help the families of those who are sick with AIDS. And poor educational opportunities, such as support for school uniforms and school books or other related studies.
- To help with family problems. Poor families. And socially disadvantaged. Have developed skills. And wellbeing. And a member of the society. Can live a normal life in society.
- To prepare the site with a friendly atmosphere. To assist people with family problems. And socially disadvantaged. And the relationship with the families of those who wish to get help.
- Through the help of a friendly, great staff and a team of people.
- To the public. Or cooperate with other charitable organizations. To the public.
- Not associated with any political process.

The mission of the Foundation:

- The integration project. "Love your home" home care for people infected with HIV to come under the administration of the Foundation.
- The website is only in Thai and they have as off 2012 April stills a Malware inside the website. So if you want to visit them or help we suggest you call them.

Contact:
Address: 77 M.8, Soi Nongmaikan 16, Nongprue, Banglamung, Chonburi 20150
Telephone: +66 38 73-0498, +66 89 606 8104
Website: http://www.gloryhutfoundation.or.th

Hand to Hand Foundation

They are a group of people from around the globe, all with different gifts, but all with the same passion: helping those who need it most, especially the exploited, neglected, and abused.

Hand to Hand works every day, one child at a time to make a difference. With people like you standing alongside them, saying "Enough! No more and never again will this child be exploited" can change be made. The problem is daunting and we know it will not be undone overnight, but any action is better than inaction so each and every move made to better a child's life makes a profound difference.

Contact:
Address: 20/149 M.10, Nongprue, Banglamung, Chonburi 20150
Telephone: +66 89 093 6067, +66 89 252 2191
Website: http://www.handtohandpattaya.org

Banglamung Boys's Home Foundation

Under a lot of population and economic pressure, it happens that the change and weakening of the structure and function of families sometimes caused difficulty for particular kinds of children to adjust themselves properly with such circumstances.

These children are orphaned, abandoned, vagrants, misbehaved etc., In order to cope the problems and strengthening the life of these unfortunate children, Banglamung Home for boys was established in 1956, is one unit belonging to the Office of Prevention and Resolution of Woman and Child Trafficking, Department of Social Development and Welfare, Ministry of Social Development and Human Security.

Objectives
- To provide residential care for boys aged between 7 - 18 years who are in need of care and protection and provision of social service, rehabilitation and educational services to enable the children to be equipped with knowledge and prepare them to become the qualified people in the society.
- To protect and develop children who are in family and community.

Services
- Full support: it is provided in terms of shelter, food, clothing, medical care and treatment, in case of serious illness, treatment at the hospital shall be arranged.
- Facilities for general and vocational education.
- Consultative service.
- Recreational service.
- Necessary services for proper development, physically, mentally and intellectually.
- Employment service after discharge or arrangement of proper placement.

Admission
- The boys aged between 7 - 18 years old.
- The orphaned, abandoned, vagrants, the boys from poor or broken families.
- Children who under adverse circumstances, cannot be looked after properly by their parent or guardians.
- Children with behavior problems.
- Children who are referred to this home by governmental and private organization concerned.

Contact:
Address: 61 M.3 Sukumvit Rd., Banglamung, Chonburi 20150
Telephone: +66 3824 1373
Website: http://www.banbanglamung.com

BACK MATTER

Bonus

If you write a review about this book on amazon.com we will give you the access to a paid forum only open to buyers of the nocovercharge.com books. Please visit http://www.nocovercharge.com/forum for more information.

Glossaries

Baht is the currency of Thailand.
Soi is a side-street branching off a major street.

About the Author

Balthazar Moreno was born on Islands in Scandinavia. His family has roots in Europe but his strong curiosity for Buddhism and Asia led him to Asia. He spent the last 12 years traveling in Asia, using Thailand as a base for his travels. After writing blogs and creating over 400 websites, he turned to Amazon to publish his first books during 2011. Balthazar is a writer, blogger, philanthropist and self made Thailand expert. When he is not writing books he enjoys charity, study Buddhism, fitness and teaching other how to live an easy simple but happier life.